A FACE IN THE CROWD

Expressions of Gay Life in America

A FACE IN THE CROWD

Expressions of Gay Life in America

Edited by John Peterson and Martin Bedogne

PROSPECT
PUBLISHING

© 2002 by John Peterson and Martin Bedogne

All rights reserved. Printed in Korea. Except as permitted under the United States Copyright Act of 1976, no part of this publication may be reproduced or distributed in any form or by any means, or stored in a database or retrieval system, without the prior written permission of the publisher.

Photo and other credits on page 133.

Every effort has been made to locate copyrighted material that appears in this book as required under copyright law. For some materials, however, the publisher has been unable to identify or locate the copyright holder. In such cases, copyright holders are invited to contact the publisher, who will be pleased to make the necessary arrangements at the first   portunity.

This book is based on photographs and information from public events, and sources believed to be reliable. Every effort has been made to make the book as complete and accurate as possible based on information available as of the printing date, but its accuracy and completeness cannot be guaranteed. Despite the best efforts of the editors and publisher, the book may contain photos of, and text about, individuals who are not gay and/or do not wish to be identified as such. The reader should use this book only as a general reference and not as the ultimate source of information about the subject of the book or the individuals contained within.

First Printing: January 2003

10 9 8 7 6 5 4 3 2 1

Library of Congress Cataloging-in-Publication Data
CIP Number Pending

Cover and interior design: Ingrid Olson, Tülbox Creative Group
Cover photograph: David La Chapelle

Prospect Publishing
P.O. Box 46753
Los Angeles, CA 90046
Visit our Web site at www.ProspectPublishing.com

A Face in the Crowd is available at special quantity discounts to use as premiums, for educational purposes, and/or sales promotions. For more information, please write to Prospect Publishing, P.O. Box 46753, Los Angeles, CA 90046 or Sales@ProspectPublishing.com.

Dedicated to young people everywhere who are living their lives with dignity, honesty, and respect. May you embrace who you are and find strength in the inspiring people you will encounter on your life's journey. They are there. Just look for that face in the crowd.

PHOTOGRAPHS BY:

Ismail Elshareef

Alex Gibson

Cheryl Haines

Alexandra Hedison

Eric Stephen Jacobs

David LaChapelle

Judy Lawne

Rob Lebow

Nanette Martin

Martha Murphy

Alan Skinner

Jay Wheeler

Kelly Wine

Albert J. Winn

Claudia Wong

A VERY SPECIAL THANKS TO:

A heartfelt thank you to Judy & Dennis Shepard, directors of the Matthew Shepard Foundation, for making this book possible. We are extremely grateful for their ongoing support and dedication.

Other members of the Matthew Shepard Foundation provided invaluable assistance and consultation. We appreciate the commitment of Tristan E. Higgins-Goodell, Christopher Maluck, Sarah McMullen, and Tina M. Nations.

We thank Betty DeGeneres for her support and participation in providing a thoughtful and heartwarming message in her foreword, and for her tireless work in advancing human rights for GLBT individuals.

Ingrid Olson of Tülbox Creative Group designed and produced this book. We salute her creative vision and thank her for her endless patience.

And to Mari Florence, we are grateful for her guidance and for sharing her extensive knowledge and experience, enabling this book to be published.

We extend a very special thanks to the following organizations and individuals for their support:

CIRE Foundation: Eric Criswell

Crossroads School: Adam Behrman & the members of Friends of Lesbians and Gays (FLAG)

Randi Driscoll, songwriter and performer of the benefit single "What Matters?"

The Gay Lesbian and Straight Education Network (GLSEN): Kevin Jennings, Eliza Byard, Scott Hirschfeld, & Christopher Ramirez

The Human Rights Campaign (HRC): Elizabeth Birch

The LGBT Community Center, National History Archive: Rich Wandel & Richard Dworkin

ONE Institute & Archives: Mark Thompson & Stuart Timmons

Project Angel Food: Jamie Natelson & Pamela Brannon

Queer Youth TV: Bret Berg, Alex Hinton, & all those who shared their personal coming-out stories in this book.

And finally, to the many individuals that provided encouragement or help along the way, we are truly grateful:

Kay Anderson	Susan Jonaitis	Roger Ritchie
Jim Andre	Judy Lawne	Roger Ritter
Susan Atkins	Debi Karolewski	Allison Seale
Karen Atkinson	Paul Kellogg	Karen Siugzda
Stanley Bochniak	Michael Kearns	Alan Skinner
Deborah Churchill Luster	Janna Kuntz	Kerry Slattery
Craig B. Coogan	Nanette Martin	Laura Stegmuller
Joe Delaplaine	Martha Murphy	Keoni Tyler
Ismail Elshareef	Rhea Murray	LaVonna Young
Jerry Gardsbane	Bruce Murray	Albert J. Winn
Alex Gibson	Michael D. Nielsen	Kelly Wine
Mary Grego	Ann Peterson	Jay Wheeler
Cheryl Haines	Charles W. Peterson, Jr.	Mark Zecca
Wendy Higgins-Goodell	Romaine Patterson	
Mira Ingram	Michael Quintos	

FOREWORD

> "Two roads diverged in a wood, and I—
> I took the one less traveled by,
> And that has made all the difference."
>
> —ROBERT FROST, from "The Road Not Taken"

"Mom, I'm gay."

Those three little words spoken to me by my daughter Ellen more than 20 years ago changed my world forever. In an instant, all that I thought I'd known about her, about myself, and about life came into question.

When my personal journey down the road less traveled began, homosexuality was not a subject that came up in 'polite' conversation—certainly not the small East Texas town in which I lived at the time. There were no P-FLAG meetings (Parents, Families and Friends of Lesbians and Gays) for support, the Internet, as we know it today, didn't exist, and there were certainly no gay role models on television. Books like *A Face in the Crowd* were essentially nonexistent. What few books were available on the subject in the public library 25 miles away, I read voraciously.

As I grappled with this new information about my daughter, some of what I went through was not unlike the grieving process that follows the death of a loved one—which is also a process of growth. Of course, what was dying wasn't a loved one, but my own expectations about the way Ellen should be. And in their place, room was being made for the truth and the new opportunities the truth would provide.

Though this process was not easy, I allowed it to take its course. Most of all, I never stopped loving my daughter, and she never stopped loving me. We kept the lines of communication open; this was vital for both of us. Among the questions I asked Ellen was, "Maybe it's a phase?"

The truth of the matter is that homosexuals do not choose their sexual orientation anymore than we heterosexuals choose ours. As I began to move from acceptance to understanding in my journey, I read all that I could on what it meant to be gay. I learned it is not any more a "lifestyle," as some people have labeled it, than being born Asian American or left handed. A person's sexual orientation is an intrinsic part of who they are as a person. Some people are born to be tall, some people are blessed with a high metabolism, and, yes, some are born homosexual.

Experts predict that as much as 3 to 10 percent of the world population is homosexual. And there are others who think 10 percent is a low figure. If that is true, then parents should face the possibility that one or more of their children could be gay. Well, I'm proud to tell you that you're in very good company.

Over the years, my family and I have been honored to get to know many people who offer love and support to their gay and lesbian children. Like me, they have come to the realization that whatever dreams they may have had for their children that didn't include them having a same-sex life partner, were simply their dreams. As you'll see in the pages that follow, it doesn't mean that their children's lives can't be happy, fulfilled, and full of love.

I'm sorry to say I've also met people who received less understanding from their parents. Tragically, some have been thrown out on the streets, beaten, and verbally abused. You'll find some of these stories on the pages that follow, as well. The truth, after all, is that both realities exist.

But one need not feel alone today when facing the realization that you or a family member is gay. Now there are vast resources on the Internet, chat rooms, support groups, books, and yes, even television role models.

I'm proud to say that Ellen's now-famous "coming out" episode in her self-named sitcom in 1997 did much to elevate the dialogue on this subject. I am reminded of a 76-year-old lesbian who wrote to Ellen and told her she never thought she'd see an openly gay lead on a TV show—and on a show done with such "poignancy, taste, and humor." Later Ellen joked in a speech that, "Being new to all this, I didn't know there were 76-year-old lesbians." *A Face in the Crowd* demonstrates how long homosexuality has been around by presenting several famous historical figures who, in addition to the various contributions they made to our society, just happened to be gay.

Many Americans have since come to recognize that homosexual men and women are not a special interest group with an "agenda;" they are simply citizens. They are citizens who should have the same basic human rights extended to all regardless of race, religion, color, or creed. There are no second-class citizens, right?

Acceptance. Tolerance. Unconditional love. These are concepts every family should regard with reverence and respect. When you and your children live these truths, you can live a life to be proud of and you can treat everyone in your family with the loving kindness they deserve.

Twenty years ago, the thought that I would be the first non-gay spokesperson for the Human Rights Campaign, be shaking hands with a President, legislators from both houses, and have authored two books of any kind— much less books that discussed homosexuality—would have seemed incredulous to say the least. But that's the fascinating thing about life: You never know what's just around the bend, particularly if you allow yourself to be open to new ideas. I look back upon the road I've traveled and see that my choice to love and support my child was not only the best choice I could have made for Ellen, but was one of the greatest gifts of my life. Hers is 'a face in the crowd' that I truly love. Enjoy the book.

Betty DeGeneres

Betty DeGeneres

INTRODUCTION

In a perfect world, this book would not exist.

There would be no need for it. Kids who played together would grow up and nurture and support each other in their adult lives. Our children would all have equal opportunities for success and happiness. Parents who love and cherish their children would do their very best to raise them into healthy, confident adults. Sadly, that world is not here yet.

When Matthew died in 1998, our family grieved at the premature loss of our son and brother. In this ideal world, Matthew would be alive, living his life and touching the lives of those around him. He had an interest in politics and current news events. He was quite adept at understanding complex issues and was equally adept at expressing his opinions on these issues. He had such hopes for the future, his future. Every new step for him meant new challenges, new friends, and new experiences.

A Face in the Crowd is an extension of Matthew's dreams. He knew that judging people before knowing them was a loss of an opportunity. He never understood why everyone did not think that way. He felt there could be nothing better on this earth than another friend. In the following pages, you will see a diverse group of people living lives filled with love, hope, and happiness. No one has the right to deny or take away the right for another person to celebrate life and show individual expressions of love simply because that person is seen as different.

The Matthew Shepard Foundation is proud to support *A Face in the Crowd*. It is our sincere desire that this book will serve an important role in our attempt to break down barriers rooted in prejudice and hate. Together, we must commit to move beyond the simple task of tolerance of those who are perceived as being different, and begin to embrace the rich diversity that exists around us. As individuals, by simply changing our lives to live it with honesty, compassion, and love, we have the ability to touch those around us in significant ways. It is a choice we make each moment of each day.

As parents, it hurts us to hear that children have been thrown out of their homes by family members who cannot, or choose not to, accept their child's very brave admission. Most children would rather come home with solid "F's" on a report card than come out to a parent as gay or lesbian. It is a brave act to stand up and proclaim who they are. Every day, 13 homeless youth die on the street. It does not have to be this way. Often the youth who find love and acceptance within their families must endure abuse and harassment perpetuated by peers in their schools, churches, or communities. We urge parents to teach their children that there is a better way.

For you the parents, who are angry with your children, or the youth, who have not given your loved ones an opportunity to support you, remember that our son, Matt, was in this world one day and then gone the next. Life and time is fleeting. Use it as best you can to heal the wounds of the past and grow forward together.

Matthew died at the hands of two young men who hated him simply because he was different. They did not know him. They did not know our family or his friends. Those who knew him continue to feel his loss. Other communities have seen similar crimes committed because of hatred for a person's skin color, religious beliefs, sexual orientation, or simply the way they looked, thought, or spoke. Hate and intolerance are learned behaviors, and do not need to be passed on to our children.

Because of the extraordinary situation surrounding his death, Matt became an international face for hate-crimes. Our quiet son became a symbol of all that is wrong in our world: hate, bigotry, ignorance, intolerance. Please help us continue to show that his voice has not been silenced in vain. Your one voice, your face in the crowd, has enormous potential to affect those around you.

We are so pleased with this book that you hold in your hands. *A Face in the Crowd* was created to illustrate to GLBT youth, their loved ones, and the general public, that there is no one specific way to live in America as a gay individual. From historic figures and role models to community and family, we hope to show that gay life in North America simply does not fit a single stereotype, that there are challenges to overcome but the future is increasingly hopeful.

If you are a gay, lesbian, bisexual, or transgender individual, we hope that you will find resonance in this book. Perhaps you are a parent or educator who can learn more about those you love and care for and will find valuable resources for self-education. You are undoubtedly a friend if you are reading this book. Share this book and the messages with your family, friends, and loved ones, or anyone else who may benefit from its positive message. Many times, the mere act of self-acceptance and sharing one's experience can have a profound influence on those around us.

Knowledge and education are the best weapons we have against intolerance. Please join us in passing on these words, and the values within, to help ensure a more accepting and safer world for our children.

Sincerely,

Judy & Dennis

Judy and Dennis Shepard

FAMILY

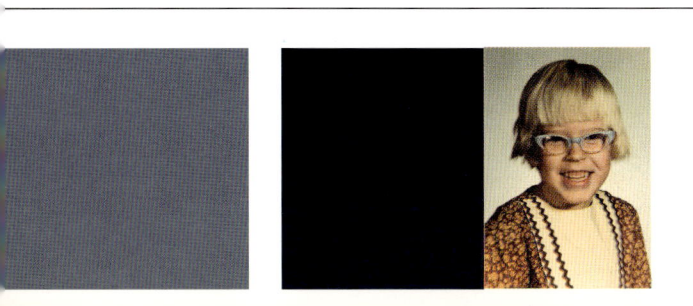

RHEA & BRUCE MURRAY

"When Bruce came out to me I was terrified.
I tried to bargain with God to change my son.

Then I realized that it was not Bruce
who needed to change, it was me."

Phil Wilson was drawn into activism by his lover Chris Brownlie. Wilson co-founded the National Black Lesbian and Gay Leadership Forum. Mayor Tom Bradley named him city AIDS coordinator in which he did battle with politicians who wanted to test restaurant workers for HIV. He became public policy director for AIDS Project Los Angeles while continuing to work for gay and lesbian civil rights, especially those involving people of color.

"Now I don't tolerate having a gay son—
I celebrate it."

Dr. Mary E. Walker, M.D., was a determined female patriot who was way ahead of her time. A Civil War physician, she was awarded the Congressional Medal of Honor in 1865. She worked as a field surgeon near the Union front lines for almost two years, then was appointed assistant surgeon of the 52nd Ohio Infantry.

Talk to your son or daughter.
Do not let your child agonize alone
over who they may be.

ALEX GIBSON

My name is Alex Gibson, a photojournalist from Los Angeles.
I am the still photographer and one of the public speakers for
the project *Out In The Cold*, a documentary on homeless queer youth.

I took pictures over a four-month period of homeless queer youth in San Francisco and Hollywood. During that time I was exposed to a world that many deny or do not know exists—one of homeless kids, living on our streets because they are lesbian, transgender, bisexual, or gay.

It is my hope that through my images, anyone reading this book will better understand a reality that affects many, not only in this country, but in the world.

Martin Duberman shocked his conservative colleagues in the early '70s by coming out in print. He was one of the first scholars to document the history of gay people, which played a major role in establishing "queer studies" as a serious and valid subject for research. He resigned from his tenured post at Princeton to open the Center for Lesbian and Gay Studies at City University of New York.

I recently came out to my parents this summer, but I did in an untraditional way. Everyone tells you not to write a letter because you're supposed to do it face-to-face. I respect that. My parents had no idea because they were always trying to set me up on dates.

You figure that every mother has an idea that their son is gay,

but my mom was in deep denial. I wrote them a letter. A part of me wanted to be there, so that when they did get news, I could answer any questions immediately and confirm anything that I said. But a part of me also didn't because you hate to see your mother cry. She said she didn't cry but I talked to her afterwards and I didn't get good vibes over the phone.

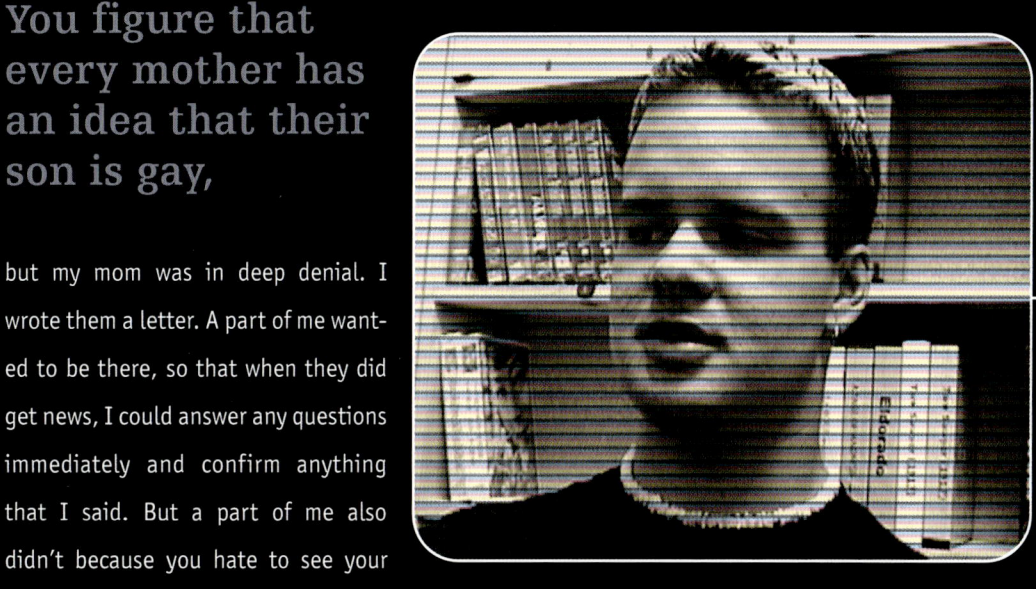

My dad was like, "Don't label yourself, you're too good for that, give girls a chance, you're missing out on the best part of life." I compromised with him and told him "I'd keep an open mind if he'd keep an open mind." I figured that was the only middle ground we could have that both of us could agree with. I think if I had been there, they might have accepted it a little bit more quickly, but I guess that being around me, seeing that I'm the same person, that I haven't changed, and I'm still their son, that's probably the best remedy.

People will tell you that there are
> only two options in life.

You can be straight
and get married or you can be who you are, and
> be excluded from their definition of family.

When the Matthew Shepard Foundation and the CIRE Foundation asked me to photograph and research the plight of homeless queer youth in America, I readily accepted the challenge. It was my opportunity to help give a voice to the numerous lesbian, gay, bisexual, and transgender youth living on the streets today.

Sal Mineo was nominated for an Academy Award for his role in *Rebel Without A Cause*, an important teenage drama of the '50s. A talented actor with numerous film, television, and stage credits, he was also an accomplished recording artist. Mineo was murdered at his Hollywood home at age 37 in 1976. His killer has never been caught.

22

Billie Jean King redefined the world of tennis when she clobbered the legendary tennis player Bobby Riggs in the "Battle of the Sexes" tennis exhibition. She was named "Outstanding Female Athlete of the World" in 1967, Sports Illustrated's "Sportsperson of the Year" in 1972 (the first woman to be so honored), and "Female Athlete of the Year" in 1973.

You've probably
    even been told
that men are "meant" to be with women,
and women are "meant" to be with men.

Who makes these rules?

Throughout this incredible journey, it was shocking to encounter so many homeless youth who were kicked out by parents who could not, or choose not, to accept their child for their sexual orientation.

Gay and lesbian families totaled 601,209 in 2000 with 304,148 gay male families and 297,061 lesbian families.

James Hormel was sworn in as the United States Ambassador to Luxembourg in 1999, becoming the first openly gay U.S. ambassador. Hormel received flack from conservative lawmakers for his out-front support of gay and lesbian rights, and a handful of key Republican senators railed against his activism. The White House ended the debate by appointing Hormel to his post while Congress was on summer recess.

The Human Rights Campaign estimates that the 2000 U.S. Census count of gay and lesbian families could be undercounted as much as 62 percent.

David Goodstein was a millionaire investment banker who was fired when it was discovered he was gay. He invested his own money and founded the Whitman-Radclyffe Foundation and sponsored numerous projects including public information and education campaigns. From 1975–1985 Goodstein, as publisher/owner of *The Advocate* hired gay writers and professionalized gay journalism.

I came out to my family when I was in my second year of college. I decided to tell my father first because we don't have the greatest relationship.

Afterwards, he thanked me for telling him first.

The summer after I came back from school, I got a phone call from someone my father went to school with. He told me that his son goes to UCLA and the four of us should go out to dinner. He suggested that I meet his son and show him around Los Angeles a bit.

I remember my father asking me if I was dating anyone and what was going on. And I thought, no I'm not dating anyone and that's a really odd question. So my dad comes and we decide to go out and meet my father's friend and his son. We're eating and his son and I decide that we should go out, grab a cup of coffee, and talk and stuff. We started to realize that we were being set up. We were on a date, and we couldn't believe it. His father had pretty much asked him the same thing—whether or not he was dating anyone.

It was really awkward. We were just taken aback by our fathers' boldness. The son and I have gone out a few more times and things have gone well. My father and I still don't necessarily have the best relationship, but it was a really sweet gesture that he hoped would bring the two of us closer.

Cleve Jones offered a profound symbol of grief in 1987 when he created a three-by-six-foot panel in his backyard to memorialize his best friend, actor Marvin Feldman. Today, the NAMES Project Foundation's Quilt spans the area of 17 football fields. Jones is the author of the book *Stitching A Revolution*.

Can you imagine being 14, 16, 19 years old, homeless, and not knowing where to turn for support?

According to the Los Angeles Gay and Lesbian Center, nearly 15,000 homeless youth sleep on the streets of Los Angeles every night. Nearly 6,000 of them identify themselves as lesbian, gay, bisexual, transgender, or "questioning."

All it takes to be a family is love,

commitment, and the desire to be together.

Rock Hudson was an actor whose celebrity status brought mainstream attention and awareness to the AIDS crisis. With his extreme good looks, Hudson became one of the leading male screen idols of the 1950s and '60s. His comedic flair was highlighted in a series of romantic comedies, often opposite Doris Day. Hudson was later popular on TV in the series *Macmillan and Wife*.

What has kept you together all these years?

"Compromise, and learning to not have
to be right all the time."

ROGER AND JERRY, TOGETHER 22 YEARS

"Trust, understanding, and a strong appreciation for
the quality of our life together."

JIM AND PAUL, TOGETHER 15 YEARS

"Wendy keeps me safe."
"Tristan makes sure my life is interesting."

TRISTAN AND WENDY, TOGETHER 12 YEARS

"We both had a willingness to try and see things
from the other's perspective. This enriched our lives,
but often times, took some work."

SUSAN AND MARCIA, TOGETHER 9 1/2 YEARS,
BEFORE SUSAN LOST MARCIA TO BREAST CANCER

Alan Turing was a British mathematician instrumental in the Allies' victory of World War II by breaking the secret German communications code, Enigma. He not only cracked the code, but his theories also opened the door to ideas that have given rise to modern computers. His refusal to live as a closeted gay man lead to his conviction of a "crime" and excluded him from further development of computers that his theories and practical application had influenced.

FLORENCE AND BOBBY, TOGETHER 43 YEARS

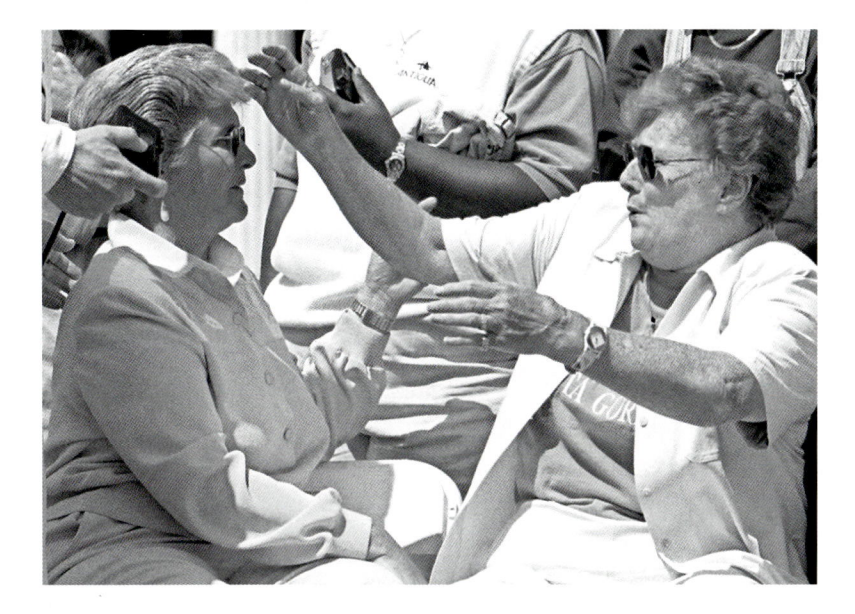

"Respect, love and understanding...and we **communicate**."

"Harry's **determination** and strength has **overcome** my impatience."

RALPH AND HARRY, TOGETHER 45 YEARS

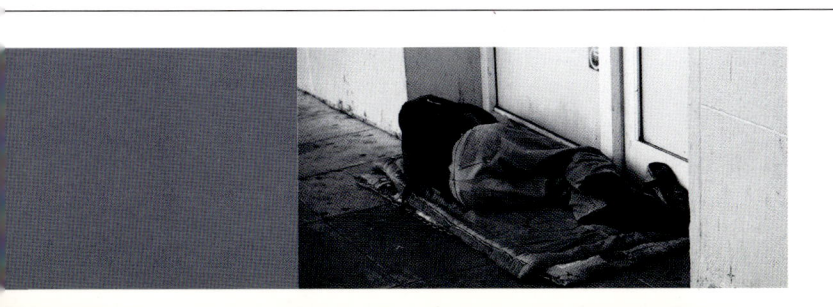

The young people I met live on the streets under harsh conditions. They have to worry about safety (rape, stabbings), being robbed of the few possessions they have, and they sleep in the cold—the sidewalk is literally their bed.

32

Field Marshall Montgomery waged war against Hitler's Nazi army during World War II. Known simply as "Monty" in every household in Britain, he was their equivalent of Douglas MacArthur or George Patton. His greatest victory came in North Africa in the fall of 1943 at the Battle of El Alamein when Montgomery's 8th army halted the advance of the Germans.

OLIVIA TORRES

The funniest part about telling my mom about liking boys and liking girls was that she always said it was okay to like girls, and that boys liking boys was no big deal. But when I actually came out to her and asked her, "Well, is it okay that I like boys and I also like girls?" She flipped out and basically took on the attitude of

"It's okay for everybody else, but not for my kid."

Her biggest difficulty was actually having it hit home.

My girlfriend used to come over when I was in high school, and we would hang out and do homework. There were a number of times when she had to sneak out of my bedroom window because it was like two o'clock in the morning and she wasn't supposed to be there. I remember my dad always loved having her come over and everything. I don't think to this day he knows that she was actually my girlfriend, but one day I'll get around to telling him.

MARGARET CHO

"I believe that a government that would
deny a gay man the right to bridal registry
is a fascist state."

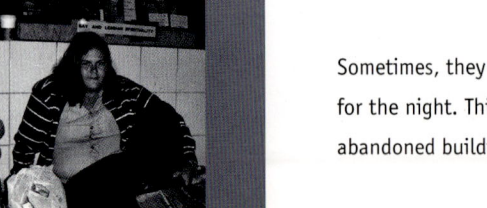

34

Sometimes, they find a "squat"—a safe place to sleep for the night. This might be under a bridge or in an abandoned building or alleyway.

Angelina Weld Grimké wrote poetry, fiction, reviews, and biographical sketches, as well as the play *Rachel*, about an African-American woman who rejects marriage and motherhood. She wrote love letters at the tender age of 16 to Marmie Burril, but she worked hard to hide her lesbianism from her father, during her life, so most of her lesbian-orientated poetry was not published until after her death. She was named after her aunt, Angelina Emily Grimké Weld, a famous abolitionist and women's rights advocate.

James Dale, a highly awarded Eagle Scout, was kicked out of Boy Scouts of America after a local newspaper article contained a speech he gave on gay adolescents. His involvement with the Boy Scouts includes both participation as a youth in the program, as well as a legal battle fighting against their anti-gay policies.

If you have a powerful urge to parent, listen to your heart.
Do not allow your identity as a gay person to prevent you from fulfilling what may be
a very organic part of who you are.

All of those I met were younger than 23 years old and some were as young as 14. They carry small bags filled with all their personal belongings.

MICHAEL & TIA KATHERINE KEARNS

"I always wanted to be a dad.
I knew I wanted to love, nurture, support, teach, and care for a child.
But being a gay dad was not a popular option."

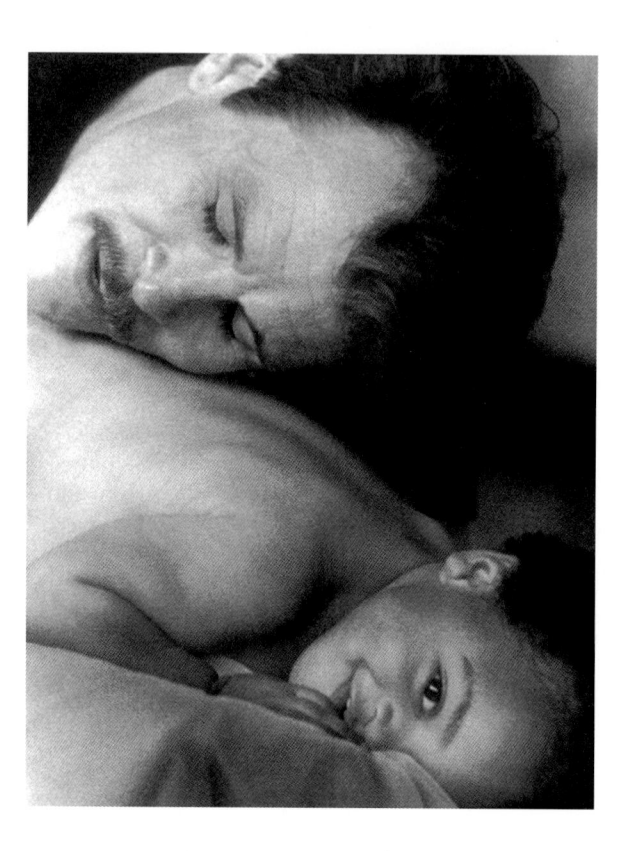

38

Within two weeks of being on the streets, most of them were introduced to drugs or prostitution, as a solution to getting money. Many cannot get jobs because of inexperience, being too young, not having clean clothes, being transgender, having warrants out for their arrest, or having no permanent mailing address.

Many seek escape through the use of drugs and eventually find themselves addicted.

"The adoption process was arduous.
I eventually became the adoptive father of an
African-American angel named Tia Katherine Kearns."

Phranc has been called the all-American Jewish lesbian folksinger. As a 17-year-old senior, she "came out" to her parents, dropped out of high school, moved to San Francisco in search of the gay community, and ended up connecting with the city's then-vital punk scene. Frustrated that punk's volume obliterated the music's lyrics, Phranc turned her talents to folk music.

Children need love, guidance, and support.

Rita Mae Brown is the author of more than a dozen novels and mysteries, several volumes of poetry, and screenplays, many of which deal with the subject of lesbianism. Her famous novel, *Rubyfruit Jungle*, broke new ground featuring a gay heroine, and her autobiography details her life as a gay activist.

It's that simple.

Not able to find jobs and unable to survive on what they were given panhandling, many resort to dehumanizing themselves through prostitution as their last resort.

Together, we must seek solutions.

I came out to my parents when I was about seventeen. I guess I hit a point in my life where I had to be out. I'm lucky because my mom has always been really supportive of everything I've done. I always looked for hints that maybe she'd be cool with it.

After I told her I was gay, there was like an hour afterwards where she was just kind of inquisitive.

How long have you known? Does anyone else know? I was like, "Yeah, a few friends know. I've known for five or six years now."

If I'd just come out to my mom, I'd still have to see my dad everyday, I'd still have to be closeted with him. Which means I'd still have to be closeted at home, and that would negate the whole point of coming out.

My father was out into the garage having a smoke. I went up to him and said, "There's something I've got to tell you." And said, "Dad, I'm gay." It's kind of funny 'cause my dad's a salesman. He's been in sales longer than I've been alive. He's got like a line for everything. But this was the only time I've ever seen him speechless. He had this cigarette in his mouth; he takes it out, blows some smoke, and says, "Really?"

My relationship with them now is infinitely better, more open than before I came out, 'cause before I was this closeted, depressed, suicidal kid who didn't want to talk to my parents about anything. But after I told them this big secret I had, I guess it just established some trust between us that allowed everything after that to blossom.

What makes a family? Love.

Jean Cocteau had an impressive influence in various art forms including poetry, novels, fashion, interior design, graphics, and film. At 17, his trip to Marseilles served as the source for his 1928 novel *The White Book*, graphically illustrated with his signature line drawings. His lover, Jean Marais, was one of the most popular French movie stars of the '40s and '50s and starred in many of Cocteau's films including *Orpheus* and *Beauty and the Beast*.

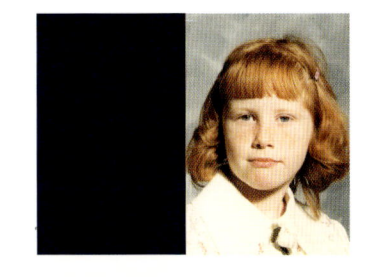

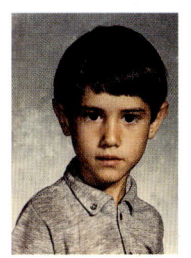

COMMUNITY

For decades, gays and lesbians kept low profiles, creating a community largely hidden from public view.

Dusty Springfield has been labeled as "only white woman who can sing soul." With a career that spans several decades and even a stint with the Pet Shop Boys on the 1987 hit "What Have I Done to Deserve This?," Springfield has cemented her role in pop music history.

The 1969 Stonewall riots served as an important historic moment in gay awareness and visibility.

David Bohnett founded GeoCities, which grew to become the largest community on the Internet, in 1994. He championed the concept of providing free home pages to everyone on the web, and he built a business model based on advertising, sponsorships, and electronic commerce. GeoCities became publicly traded on NASDAQ in 1998, and was acquired by Yahoo! Inc. in May 1999. He created the David Bohnett Foundation, which provides grants to organizations for lesbian and gays, AIDS services, gun control, and voter registration. He has been recognized as one of *Time* Digital's Top 50 Cyber Elite, one of *Upside* magazine's Elite 100, and one of *Newsweek's* "100 People to Watch in the Next Millennium."

LAVONNA & SHORTY

I met LaVonna and Shorty over a year ago on Santa Monica Boulevard.
It took me three months to realize that LaVonna was transgender.
We became friends and their story is amazing.

But it was the emergence of AIDS that further propelled gays and lesbians into **public advocacy.**

Robert Mapplethorpe is one of the most influential erotic artists ever. Often deemed obscene, his photographs were banned in Washington, D.C. He is now known as a world-renowned artist, and died of AIDS in 1989.

50

As well as **prompting others**
to take action.

Jim Kepner was a pioneer gay activist, journalist, historian, and founder of the International Gay and Lesbian Archives. Starting out as a prize-winning Bible student, he announced plans to be a missionary in Africa when interviewed by Walter Cronkite at age 12. In high school, he began questioning his beliefs, then relocated to San Francisco to explore his youthful feeling of attraction to men. He explored public libraries for every bit of information he could find on same-sex love. Finding very little, he began searching other sources, and made it his life's mission to uncover, preserve, and disseminate the true history of lesbian and gay people.

AMANDA SMITH

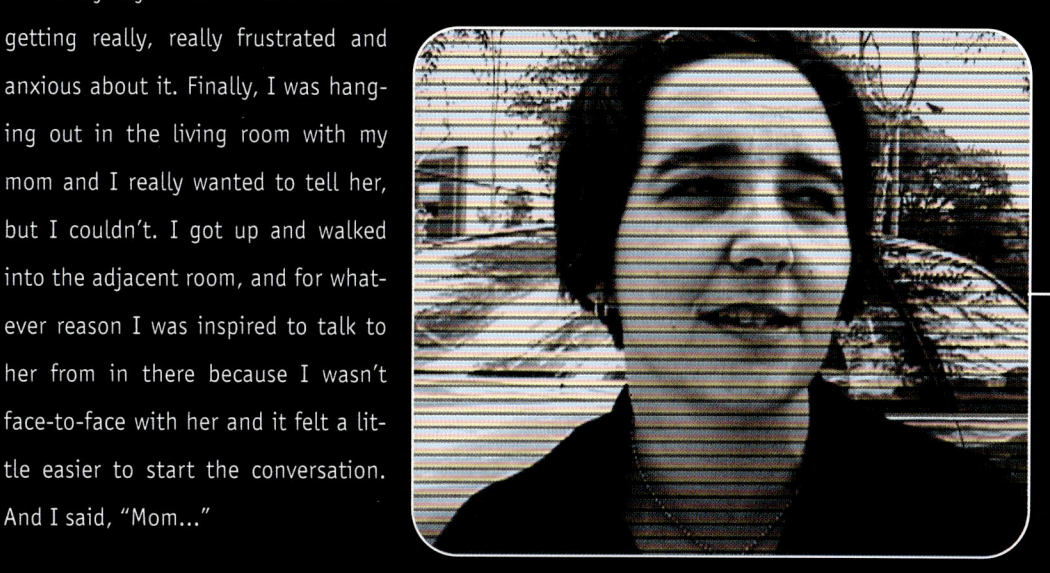

I came out when I was 23. I grew up in a pretty conservative town in Alabama. I moved out here to Los Angeles and finally found what I thought was my home community. I found gay people and a pretty supportive group of friends. I even joined a soccer team that was preparing to play in the 1986 gay games.

I went back to Alabama for a couple of weeks. I was preparing to tell my mom in particular. Every day I would wake up and say, "I'm going to tell my mom today." And every day I would chicken out. I was getting really, really frustrated and anxious about it. Finally, I was hanging out in the living room with my mom and I really wanted to tell her, but I couldn't. I got up and walked into the adjacent room, and for whatever reason I was inspired to talk to her from in there because I wasn't face-to-face with her and it felt a little easier to start the conversation. And I said, "Mom..."

I remember getting all choked up and I was really emotional and started crying.

My mom heard the fear in my voice and she came running into the room. I said, "I have something I want to tell you. I'm really worried about telling you, but I feel I have to and I just want you to know. And that is that I'm gay."

Dorothy Arzner was the first woman to join the newly formed Directors' Guild of America in 1927. She directed Paramount's first sound film, *Wild Party* and her career spanned 25 years. After her retirement, Arzner initiated the first filmmaking course at the Pasadena Playhouse, filmed numerous Pepsi Cola commercials at Joan Crawford's request, and taught at UCLA's Film Department.

Participating in the community is more than simply **showing up.**

It's **giving back.**

LaVonna and Shorty were together for a year and a half living on the streets in West Hollywood. LaVonna was kicked out of her mother's home for being a transgender three years prior to meeting Shorty.

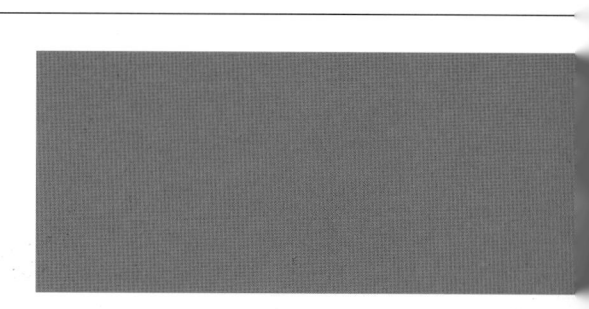

LAURA STEGMULLER

"Melissa Etheridge's song 'Scarecrow' about Matthew Shepard's murder made a powerful impact on the way my school addresses gay, lesbian, bisexual, and transgender concerns. It provided me the strength to become the first openly lesbian teacher in our district."

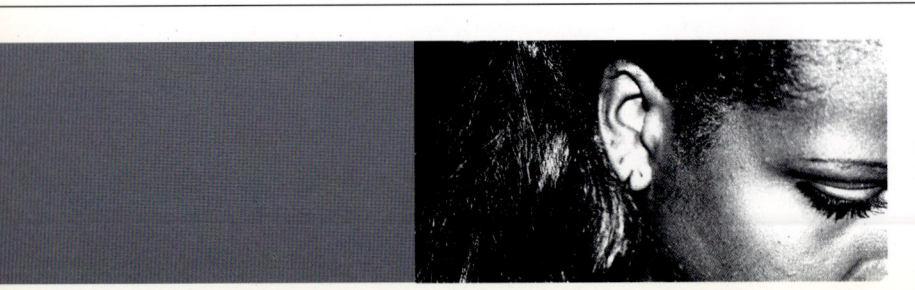

"I just want my mom to open her eyes and be proud of me. She just doesn't understand. For years, she treated me like I was wrong, like I don't know who I am. I know who I am. I'm proud of who I am."

"So far, I have had the **support of my students** and their parents, and anticipate **nothing less.**"

Rosie O'Donnell, comedienne, actress, talk show host, author and now America's most famous "gay parent" is also the host of the syndicated show "The Rosie O'Donnell Show" and the editor-in-chief of the self-titled *Rosie* magazine.

56

Patricia Nell Warren is an author and political activist. Her most successful novel, *The Front Runner*, was first published in 1974 and has become a very popular gay love story. Her novels have been favorites with young people who are struggling with coming out, or who simply want positive information about gay life.

Remember one important thing—

you are not alone.

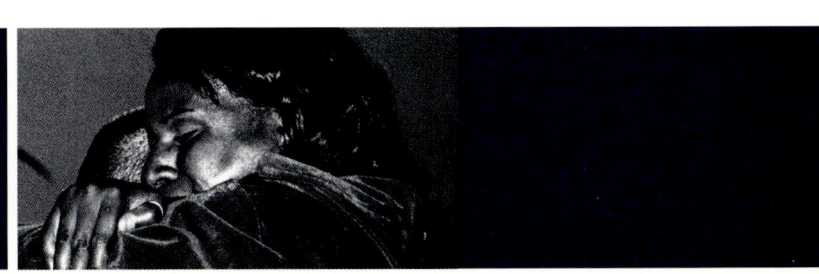

57

"The first night I slept on the street, Shorty asked 'are you scared?' I said 'no.' He said 'close your eyes and tuck your head into my chest.' It made me feel safe."

Some people explore spirituality.

Many return to their faith,
or simply rediscover it.

"I see a lot of problems with the gay kids out here—most left home for fear of their parents. It's pretty bad when your own family calls you a faggot, a punk, a devil's child. Why hate somebody for being who they are? If they''re being real— love 'em."

Reverend Mel White has served as ghostwriter of autobiographies of such anti-gay promoters as Jerry Falwell and Pat Robertson. A drastic transformation took place for White after Falwell claimed that AIDS was God's punishment on homosexuals. He came out with the book *Stranger At The Gate: To Be Gay and Christian in America*, became dean of the Cathedral of Hope Metropolitan Community Church in Dallas, and founded his own social justice ministry, Soulforce.

One of the difficulties of coming out was my religion. A lot of people ask me, "But aren't you Christian?" I'll say, "Yeah, why is that relevant?" A lot of people don't recognize the fact that to be gay doesn't necessarily mean that you're not religious, and that there's really no conflict between the two.

I am Episcopalian. It's a particular flavor of Christianity that is quite similar to Catholicism, but remarkably different in a few areas. The doctrines state that you should do what you believe is true, rather than just blindly doing what you're told. It's been my experience that a lot of churches tell you what to believe and how to behave. They don't explain it or let you arrive at your own conclusions. In the Episcopal Church, if you have a different opinion, they'll say, "That's interesting." Not that

Some come to realize that the God they
believe in could never condemn
them for being who they truly are.

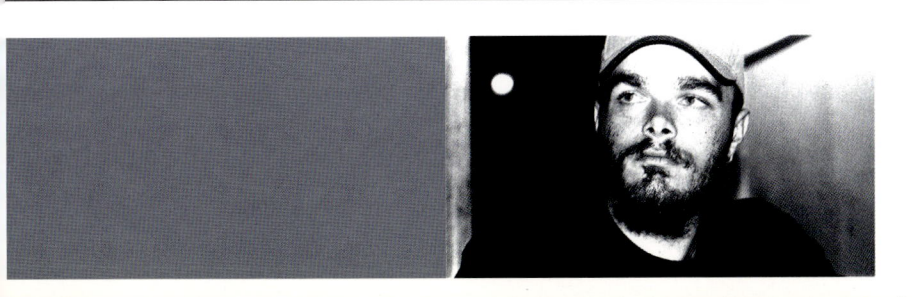

"We've been hanging out on the streets here in West Hollywood. It's the safest place, and there's more money—people seem willing to help you if you are a good person."

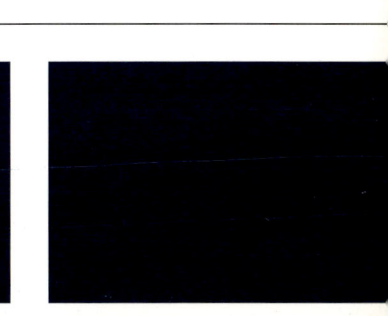

In the 1960s, a group of gay men came together and called themselves the Radical Faeries.

Hans Christian Andersen had poetry and prose published and plays produced beginning in 1822. His first novel, *The Improviser*, was well received, and his first book of fairy tales was published that same year. Andersen's tales of fantasy include "The Ugly Duckling," "The Emperor's New Clothes," "The Snow Queen," "The Red Shoes," and "The Little Mermaid." Andersen traveled extensively and continued to write novels, plays, and travel books, but it was his more than 150 stories for children that established him as one of the great figures of world literature.

They used drag as a means to challenge both traditional views of masculinity and traditional views of homosexuality.

Sir Ian McKellen is an actor with a career so distinguished he was knighted by Queen Elizabeth. His Shakespearean performances on stage and screen are legendary and his versatility in modern work, as well as the classics has earned him numerous acting awards. His portrayal of the wizard Gandalf in *The Lord of the Rings: The Fellowship of the Ring* earned him the Screen Actors Guild award for Best Supporting Actor and a nomination for the Academy Award®. Several years ago, he outed himself during a BBC broadcast and is a co-founder of Stonewall, an organization that strives for equality for gays and lesbians.

An important early influence was Harry Hay, who founded the Mattachine Society, one of the earliest gay liberation organizations in the United States.

One day, LaVonna snuck into the Metropolitan Community Church, a well-known primarily gay church in the area, and got caught by the pastor playing the piano and singing. He asked her to play for a service, then a concert.

"I never thought I'd be singing gospel music. But I am, and I love it."

Among many of Hay's ideas was the concept that
gay men were different from straight men and
that these differences should be acknowledged and accepted.

Bayard Rustin was a civil rights activists and political strategist who organized the 1963 March on Washington and influenced Martin Luther King Jr. and his monumental "I Have A Dream" speech.

The term gay "lifestyle" is often used to trivialize our experience.

It's not a lifestyle.

It's a life.

"I just hope that through my music I can help these kids out here understand that they are not wrong."

LaVonna was able to eventually leave the streets and got an apartment by taking advantage of services in Hollywood. But unfortunately, in order for LaVonna to continue her own successful journey and live a full and productive life, she had to separate from Shorty, who was not able to get off the streets.

I wanted
to kiss her.

Then in my senior year, I was taking a
psychology class and one of the exer-
cises we had to do was this story telling
project. There was a bag; the outside of
the bag represented things we tell
everybody and the inside was our personal thoughts. On the inside of the
bag, I put that I was a lesbian, and

Today LaVonna is an outreach worker for homeless queer youth for GLASS (Gay and Lesbian Adolescent Social Services) in Los Angeles. Now she is able to help those that were much like her only a short time ago.

Community and a sense of belonging can be found in many places.

Rupert Everett's break as an actor came about with the success of the international film *Another Country* in 1984. His candor about the time he spent as a hustler and his sexuality did not deter his success. His appearance in *My Best Friend's Wedding*, opposite Julia Roberts, made him a household name, making him one of the few openly gay actors.

70

Peter ILyich Tchaikovsky was a leading Russian composer whose ballet, *The Nutcracker*, contains some of the most beloved music ever written.

Sometimes you have to look for it,

and sometimes it finds you.

Keith Haring's cartoonish icons of barking dogs, radiant babies, and flying saucers began to circle the globe soon after he began installing them publicly as chalk drawings in subway cars. A one-man show in 1982 launched his commercial art world success. When diagnosed with AIDS, Haring openly discussed his illness with the press and established the Keith Haring Foundation to support both children's and AIDS-related charities.

My mother was visiting a couple days ago and she brought me a newspaper. It was *Dear Abby,* and it was this guy in Houston who came out, came out to his parents, or to his mother. He had a boyfriend and they weren't accepting of it, and they basically told him that as long as he was going to be gay, they didn't want to have anything to do with him. Another woman had read this *Dear Abby* and wrote to say that she was appalled at what his parents had done—that it was just horrible. She and her husband had two sons that both happened to be straight, and that if this young man was reading her letter that she wanted to adopt him. Be it a legal adoption or even if just by word or deed.

Even if your parents don't respond in the most wonderful way, there are plenty of people out there who are willing to be a surrogate family.

Don't give up hope just because your blood family doesn't accept it. There are plenty of people out there who will accept you for who you are.

Community is not just something you join.

It's what you make of it.

Radclyffe Hall was an out lesbian and famous British novelist who published the novel *The Well of Loneliness* in 1928, which was ruled as "obscene" in some areas after a trial due to its lesbian content.

CHALLENGES

MIRA INGRAM

"When I was growing up in Orange County, I felt alone. I didn't know other 'out' people. Then one day I learned a classmate from high school committed suicide—because he was gay."

Michelangelo created some of the most famous sculptures, paintings, and architecture in the world.

"I moved away and became politically active, but I eventually came back. I speak out now about queer issues so that others don't have to feel isolated like I did. And I hope to make a difference. There is no reason for a life to be lost simply because that person is gay."

Vito Russo was a writer, activist, and founding member of the Gay and Lesbian Alliance Against Defamation. His book *The Celluloid Closet* was later made into a documentary by Robert Epstein and Jeffrey Friedman. The power of his art and activism still have a strong influence today.

Life is certainly more challenging if you are gay, lesbian, bisexual, or transgender.

OUT IN THE COLD

What worries me most about these kids on the street is that they get comfortable with their situation and see no other way of life. They never expected to end up on the street, but they do the best they can to survive.

Morris Kight received a call in 1970 after the Stonewall Riots to organize a West Coast Stonewall Pride Parade to coincide with the March in New York. The June parade down Hollywood Boulevard was dubbed Christopher Street West. Today it draws crowds of 250,000 in West Hollywood.

It takes a great deal of courage...

...to honor your self-identification

and own experience of love.

Harry Hay gathered with four friends in the '50s to contemplate "the meaning and intent of being gay." This group became The Mattachine Society, and in the '70s he formed the Radical Faeries.

I thought it would be easier to tell them I was bisexual instead of being gay. Kind of like, I'm not totally gay, just halfway there.

I left them a note saying, "I'm bisexual." I remember all three of my brothers came to me with the note and they were like, "Is this true? Are you really gay?" My older brother was like, "I could understand if you were gay. People are born that way, but bisexual, that's just being greedy." So then I had to tell them I really was gay, not bisexual. For some reason they didn't think bisexuality existed. Either like you're gay, or you're not gay. It worked against me, and I thought it

Sappho was an immensely famous lyric poet who has been loved throughout the ages for the beauty of her writing. She lived on the island of Lesbos, from which we get the word lesbian.

Some might say that you need to change,
but there is no evidence that people
can change their sexual orientation.

They begin to think they deserve this suffering. If they turn to drugs for escape, this often leads to their demise. The streets and this type of life is brutal and unforgiving.

I was living with my father at the time. I was 18 going on 19. I came out to him and my stepmother with pretty much no problem at all.

It was my mother who had the big problem though. She was living on the East Coast at the time. I called her and the first thing she said was, "I'm sorry, you're going to die of AIDS and burn in hell." I hung up the phone and I didn't talk to my mother for a long time, for about two years. She would send me religious articles and different sorts of letters talking about how Jesus would save me, and stuff like that. She was getting heavily into her Southern Baptist religion. Basically, I told her if she kept sending this stuff I wasn't going to talk to her at all.

After about two years, she came to her senses, or we've reached a sort of agreement and basically she accepted me.

Even though she's still a Southern Baptist and heavily involved with the church, she's met my current partner. We've been together about seven years, and she accepts him. Everything's fine. We don't talk about a lot of stuff. We have a nice relationship, and everything's fine.

85

Maybe those filled with hate and rage

are the ones who should change.

Alexander the Great overthrew the Persian Empire and extended his rule from Greece to Egypt and all the way to India. His achievements laid the foundation for the powerful Roman Empire.

MARGARETHE CAMMERMEYER

"We have all been the victims of homophobia."

"In the military, you are a victim of homophobia by the 'don't ask, don't tell' policy that continues to exist."

What impresses me most about these youth is their kindness. Most of them are extremely open to being photographed and seem happy to tell their story to someone who will listen with compassion and, most importantly, with respect.

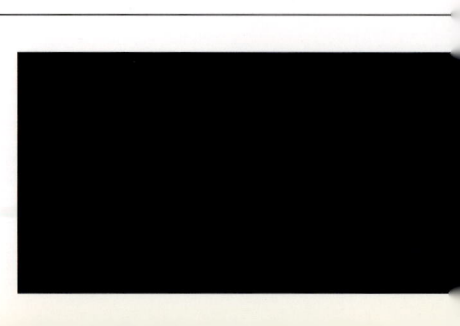

"Every time we march, there are radical people who say that fags belong in hell."

87

Greg Gorman started out as a photojournalist, shooting rock concerts in the '60s. He elevated commercial photography to the level of art with his portraits of numerous legendary pop icons. His work has been featured in various publications including *Vanity Fair*, *Vogue*, and *Rolling Stone*, as well as several coffee-table books.

MARK ZECCA & ISMAIL ELSHAREEF

"Ismail received asylum in the U.S. because of the atrocities happening in Egypt against gay men. That ensures that we will be able to stay together in this country."

Tennessee Williams is author of well-known plays including *A Streetcar Named Desire*, *The Glass Menagerie*, and *Cat on a Hot Tin Roof*.

"Other bi-national couples are not so lucky.

Work and tourist visas are only temporary solutions and offer no guarantee.
Far too often, bi-national couples must separate when their partner is forced to leave,
or they must both uproot their lives and immigrate to another county
that validates their relationship."

The problems that homeless lesbian, gay, bisexual, and transgender youth encounter extend beyond the lack of acceptance from their parents and families. Many endured harassment in the schools, churches, and their community.

90

Remember, prejudice and hate are

learned behaviors passed on to our children.

No one is born intolerant.

In a study conducted with 194 lesbian, gay, and bisexual youth aged 14 to 21 attending social and support groups in 14 metropolitan areas, it was estimated that 27 percent had been physically hurt by another student. Teenage students, both gay and straight alike, confirm that being called 'gay' is considered one of the worst harassments in today's school environment.

Many young runaways go to Hollywood, San Francisco, New York, or other major metropolitan cities. There is a certain mystique that lures them.

RYAN FOX

What mattered most was when I came out to my parents. I was away at school and I wanted to make sure it went right so I called ahead. I said, "I need time with you." I got there and my dad was asleep because he had to go to work that night—but my mom didn't tell me that. My brother was there with his friend, so none of it worked. I tried to get the friend to go home and get my mom out of the house, just so I could talk to her privately.

We drove around and then we drove to the park. I sat in my car, which is the place I've come out to so many of my friends, so it seemed kind of natural to me. I started talking to her, and I was having a really hard time getting it out and she knew I was having a hard time. I thought she knew what I was going to say. By the end of it, I had calmed her down, but she was still having a problem with it. She had all sorts of misconceptions about being gay and how I would be treated.

I was trying to tell her that I was already out and happier in my new life, but it was difficult.

So, my dad gets up, he's going to go to work at midnight. I said, "Dad I need to talk to you." He's like, "Well, okay, go ahead." I'm like, "No we need to leave." My brother was there and I didn't want to do it near my mom 'cause she would be freakin' out. So we got in the car and I stated it really simply, that I was gay. He just said, "Yeah, I thought you was." I was like, "Damn." He'd thought about it and he'd made comments when I was younger about me having a boyfriend or girlfriend, like thinly veiled things that freaked me out at the time, but at least it led me to believe that he'd be okay with it, or at least that he'd anticipated it.

It's been about two years now since I've come out to them, and they're both improving a lot. I can talk to them about things. My dad and I have gotten a lot closer, and he can tell me about things that bother him too, 'cause I think he respects me for being able to come out to him.

RHEA & BRUCE MURRAY

"At church, the minister started asking other families
if they could verify Bruce was gay.
Kids would tell us, 'Even the minister thinks you're a faggot.' "

John Boswell, a historian with training in several languages, brought a rare expertise to gay studies and challenged accepted theology. His book *Christianity, Social Tolerance and Homosexuality* provided persuasive evidence that the Christian church had not always condemned same-sex partnership. Boswell died of complications from AIDS in 1994.

"This lead to us being ostracized from our church and our community."

They think they can go to these well-known cities and find a welcome party waiting for them because they are out and proud of who they are. Instead, they find little welcome as they begin to face harsh realities.

These are everyday kids. Most of them never graduated from high school. Many lack training and experience on how to seek employment, or face challenges due to being under age with no verifiable residence.

Sadly, over 50 percent of national youth servicing organizations report that they do not have services or resources in place to educate youth on sexual orientation or to support gay and lesbian youth specifically.

The anxiety you might be feeling is normal.
Often it comes from family or social prejudice.
Or the stigma that may be associated with it.

Regardless of the messages out there,
remember that it's okay to be yourself.

Marlon Riggs was a filmmaker whose documentary *Tongues Untied* stirred a controversy over public arts funding.

My dad is also gay and when I came out to him, I thought he would be the most supportive, but he was actually the most disappointed. He was upset at me for being gay because he had grown up denying it for so long, and it was so hard on him that he just didn't want me to go through the same thing. That was really, really disappointing to me. But my mom on the other hand—whose reaction I was afraid of because she had married a man, had a child, then found out he'd been hiding that he was gay the whole time, and destroyed her family—she had no problem with it. We were in the middle of watching television and a commercial came on and I said,

"Mom, you know I'm gay?" and she was like, "Yeah, I was just waiting for you to say something."

And we were like cool and we went back to eating, and that was the whole thing with my mom.

Now my mom is my most staunch supporter of anyone in my life and my dad and I still are more friends than anything. But I just found it odd that he was so disappointed. And that hurt.

Don't be afraid to **stand up** and let your voice be heard.

Many of these homeless youth are frustrated and simply want to be heard. I hope that my photographs and interviews give them a face and a voice so the rest of us will open our hearts and compassion to them.

FUTURE

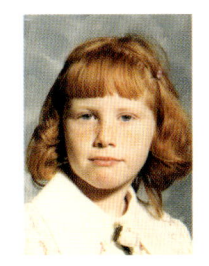

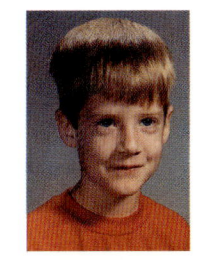

Today's youth are much more aware of the gay, lesbian, bisexual, and transgender experience than any generation before.

These individuals are often their friends, classmates, and brothers and sisters—as well as themselves.

Emily Elizabeth Dickinson was a 19th century poet who had only ten poems published during her lifetime. After her death, over 1,700 poems were discovered. The fame of her poetry has spread and she is now acclaimed throughout the world. For many years after her death, her words of love for Kate Scott and her sister-in-law, Sue Gilbert, were downplayed by her family.

Ellen DeGeneres, comedienne, actor and writer, made headlines and history in April of 1997 with her now famous "coming-out" episode on her self-titled television series. The first openly gay star of a sitcom, Ellen has become one of the most active advocates for gay, lesbian, bisexual, transgender, or "questioning" youth today.

Youth are speaking out in greater numbers than ever before.
Many make their voice heard through protest.

GERRY

I came across a boy sleeping on the sidewalk, against the wall of a building.
Everyone seemed to be walking by him. Some stop and look for a moment,
but most seem not to notice.

Others voice their outrage with silence.

Harvey Milk was the first openly gay official elected in a major city when he was voted in to the San Francisco Board of Supervisors in 1977. His mission was to be the voice of the unheard community. Milk stood up against racism, sexism, ageism, and hatred of any kind. He was instrumental in the acceptance of a gay rights ordinance and the rejection of the "Briggs Initiative" which would have banned homosexual teachers.

JOE DELAPLAINE

104

"When I was younger, I was afraid to speak out, especially on gay issues. But connecting with others gives you a lot of courage and keeps you from feeling alone."

Michael Callen was briefly featured with the Flirtations singing in the film *Philadelphia* in Tom Hanks and Antonio Banderas' Halloween party scene. Callen co-founded the People with AIDS Coalition, the Community Research Initiative, and the PWA Health Group. Through his 1990 book, *Surviving AIDS*, the singer saved millions of anonymous lives through his persistence to promote the concept of responsible "safe sex."

"No matter how you choose to express yourself—do something.

You can't do it wrong and it doesn't have to be perfect.
 Just talking with your friends is a victory. Define yourself or someone else will."

Later that evening, he is panhandling in front of a store. I put some change in his tin box and we spend the next six hours together. He tells me a little about his world. His name is Gerry.

In April of 2002, almost **2,000 schools** participated in the Day of Silence, with over 100,000 American students **choosing silence** over intolerance.

PAJAMA BINGO!
APR 12 7-10PM

APR 10 2002
STUDENTS SPEAK OUT
NAT'L DAY OF SILENCE
WWW.DAYOFSILENCE.ORG
STONEWALL LIBRARY

GLCC

Gerry was kicked out of his mother's house three years ago at age 17 for being gay/bisexual. His mother could accept her daughter being gay, but for some reason, not her son.

Gerry survives on the street through prostitution. He told me about his "sugar daddies" who want to take care of him.

Nine out of ten youth involved

were straight-identified.

Sheila James Kuehl, now in her third legislative term in the California State Assembly, is the chair of the Assembly Judiciary Committee. She was the first woman in California history to be named Speaker pro Tempore, and is also the first openly gay or lesbian person to be elected to the California Legislature.

journal in a drawer. I didn't think my parents would read it. But when I came home that night, my dad had read it, and he was very upset.

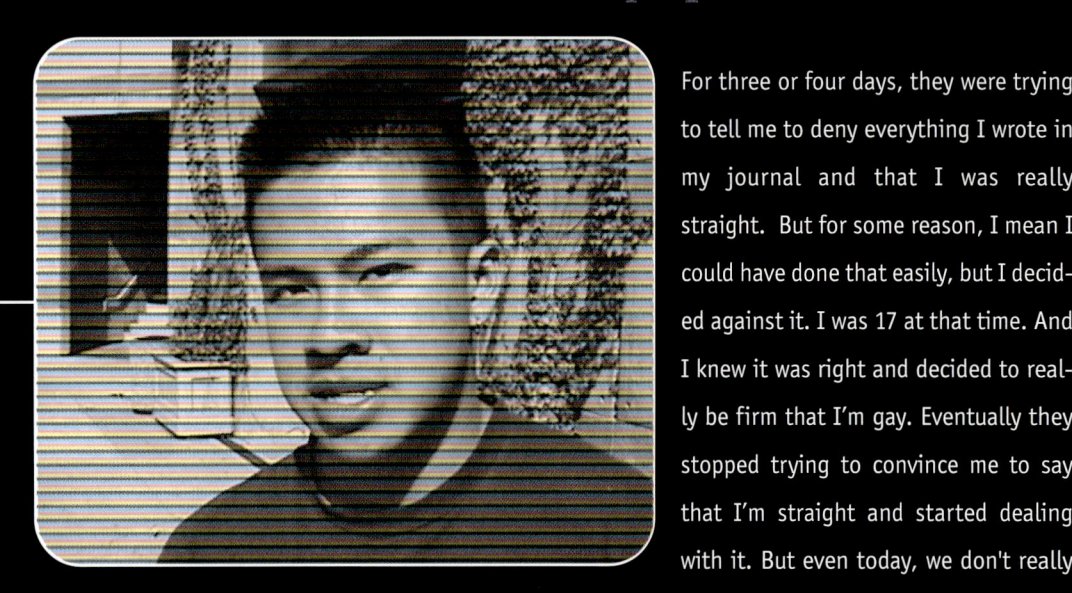

For three or four days, they were trying to tell me to deny everything I wrote in my journal and that I was really straight. But for some reason, I mean I could have done that easily, but I decided against it. I was 17 at that time. And I knew it was right and decided to really be firm that I'm gay. Eventually they stopped trying to convince me to say that I'm straight and started dealing with it. But even today, we don't really talk about it, and I don't think there's much growth on their part. But personally, my growth has been incredible. I just feel like I'm light years away from where I was two years ago. Really, two years isn't a long time, but so much growth has happened! I have all these great gay friends and it's really empowering.

Completely conceived and organized by students,
the Day of Silence Project **protests harassment** against gay youth.

109

In the place of words, students pass out cards that say, "Think about the voices you are not hearing today. What are you going to do to **end the silence?**"

George Platt Lynes is a key figure in the history of photography. He found commercial success in the '30s and '40s by taking fashion and dance photographs and portraits. Despite his fame, Lynes' true passion was photographing male nudes—a dangerous and criminal undertaking in those times. He is often considered the forefather of artists Bruce Weber, Herb Ritts, and Robert Mapplethorpe.

Franklin Kameny, a World War II veteran, was fired in 1957 from his job with the U.S. government because of his "alleged homosexuality." Kameny fought back and took his case to the Supreme Court, but further review was declined. In his attempt to attack the idea that homosexuality is an illness, Kameny disrupted a meeting of the American Psychiatric Association in 1971, accusing it of victimizing gays. He was the first openly gay person to run for U.S. Congress and was a founder of the National Gay and Lesbian Task Force and the Gay Rights National Lobby.

With love, encouragement, and support, youth are empowered
to come out earlier and feel pride in who they really are.

Don't all kids deserve this right?

"When hustling, it's kind of cool," he told me, "getting picked up off the streets and stepping into a life of luxury."

Some of Gerry's customers cook for him, give him money, take him to fancy restaurants, buy him drinks and clothes. I noticed his clothes were quite clean. Now I knew why.

Christopher Rice, the son of novelist Anne Rice, made his authorial debut at age 22 with his book *A Density of Souls*.

BRENT JAIMES

The thought of coming out was something that was always on my mind, always in my head. Everything seemed to revolve around it, and that kind of told me it was time. Before I did it, I wanted to make sure I was financially prepared. I imagined that the worst-case scenario was that I would be kicked out of the house. I don't know why I thought that. My mother never talked about anybody being gay or gave me any indication as to how she would react. But I just figured that's the worst that could happen and I wanted to be ready.

One day I was talking to my Mom about something and I didn't actually say the word gay, because I wasn't happy with the word and I couldn't articulate it very well. I said something to let her know something was up.

She went through a couple possibilities: drugs, something, I don't know, and she got to asking me if I was gay and I said yes. That's the easiest way to do it and she said, "Oh, shit" and had a cigarette.

After I came out and told my Mom, I had broken down that barrier between me and coming out to everybody else. So then I just started coming out to this little hierarchy I had of friendships. So my Mother was at the top, and I got her out of the way, and then I could go to my next closest friend and my next closest friend. Eventually I just started sending out e-mails and things like that.

LAVONNA YOUNG

"I never thought that I would **find myself homeless** for being honest about who I am, but if I can get myself off the streets, **anybody can.**

My **drive to succeed,** to just get out of my situation, is the motivating force that helped. It's important to **concentrate** on the good things that you have in your life.

If you dwell on the negative around you, **it will hold you down.**"

In return, Gerry would give them sex. He wouldn't stay long in their homes though, because he didn't trust them. He's more comfortable on the street. He has regulars. He said it rarely took him longer than a half an hour to get a 'trick.'

E.M. Forster was born in England in 1879. His novels have been popularized through several film adaptations including *Howard's End*, *A Room with a View*, *A Passage to India*, and the gay-themed *Maurice*.

When I was about 13, my mom found some cheesy gay magazines when she was changing my sheets. It was so typical because it reminded me of something that would happen to a straight boy, like his mother finding a Hustler or Penthouse underneath or between the mattresses, just like an after school special.

> I came home from school and she had this really distraught look on her face so we sat down and had "the talk."

It was really horrible because she had the magazine with her and I was like, "God, not only am I embarrassed because I'm gay, but it's such a bad magazine." I told her I was gay and now my mom is overly accepting. She embodies all the aspects of the gay male now more than I do—with her little black convertible Miata. She has tons of gay friends now. She's like a big fag hag now. She really dove into the role I guess.

In support of themselves and others, gay/straight alliances are rapidly growing at the middle school and high school level.

Kids get it.

Gerry became addicted to crack and marijuana early on. For ten dollars, he can buy a vial of crack and smoke it right there on the street.

"The cops would rather you smoke on the street than in the alleyways," he said. "They're more concerned with the people that sell it." He wants to stop taking drugs, but it's hard.

CROSSROADS SCHOOL FOR ARTS & SCIENCES
SANTA MONICA, CALIFORNIA

ADAM BEHRMAN, STUDENT ADVISOR

"At Crossroads, our high school students produced a play in support of local gay youth."

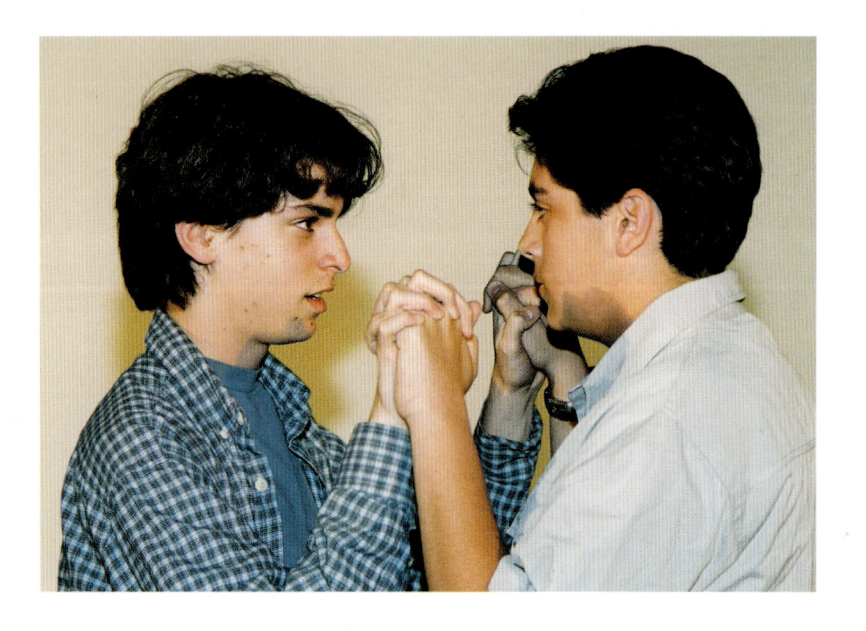

Larry Kramer is an activist and an Oscar-nominated screenwriter and novelist. In addition to the Gay Men's Health Crisis, the first grassroots AIDS service organization in the county, he was involved with the formation of the first AIDS hotline and the AIDS Coalition to Unleash Power (ACT UP), which made Silence = Death a household phrase.

"This was their way of helping other youth who are often unsupported. Support, compassion, and friendship levels the breeding ground for intolerance."

Philip Johnson is an influential modernist architect with a postmodern style.

QUEER YOUTH TV
BRET BERG & ALEX HINTON

"I became increasingly concerned about the lack of solid educational resources for queer youth on the web. I decided to personally do something about that and formed Queer Youth TV.

Alex Hinton and I videotape young people telling us their most interesting coming out stories.

Our goal is to bring more visibility to the various aspects of the gay community. But unfortunately, more visibility doesn't necessarily mean more acceptance."

David Mixner worked as a political consultant to former President Clinton and is the author of the book *Stranger Among Friends*. Mixner's early advocacy prompted ANGLE (Access Now for Gay and Lesbian Equality) to endorse Clinton in his presidential bid and raised the profile for the "gay" vote.

"We're interested in stories of empowerment and in giving queer youth a vehicle to express themselves—both openly and honestly."

Fred Schneider is one of the co-founders of the B-52's and rode through the pop era of the '80s as their lead singer. The B-52's lost guitarist Ricky Wilson to AIDS, but rebounded with commercial success. Schneider has helped expand awareness with regards to AIDS, sexuality, and animal rights.

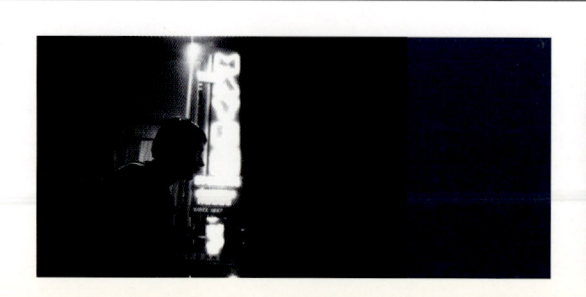

Our evening ended when a BMW pulled up and Gerry got in.
It was time for him go back to work.

Tolerance for others leads to greater civic involvement for many youth.

It's trite, but true.

Today's youth are tomorrow's leaders.

Edmund White's coming-out novel, *A Boy's Own Story*, is considered a classic of modern America fiction. White is a respected scholar and critic who helped found the Gay Men's Health Crisis in New York—the first volunteer group to fight what was then being called the "gay cancer." His works document gay life encompassing everything from the conservative '50s to the '80s.

ROMAINE PATTERSON

"My friend, Matthew Shepard, taught me the most valuable lesson of my life. He used to believe that we all had a role to fulfill in making our world and society a better place—no matter how big or small that role may be."

Elton John is a singer and songwriter, who since coming out has donated both time and money to fighting AIDS and raising visibility of gays and lesbians.

"I created the Angels Network as a way for a group of people to stand up and say, 'we can make a difference by showing what love is all about.' Why wouldn't you show the difference between love and hate if given the chance?"

Tom Stoddard was an American Civil Liberties Union lawyer and director of the LAMBDA Legal Defense Fund. He devoted much of his life to equal rights for gays, lesbians, and people with AIDS. He developed one of the first courses on sexual orientation discrimination and viewed the gay rights movement as a "subset of the Civil Rights Movement." He died of AIDS-related complications at age 48.

RESOURCE GUIDE

SUPPORT ORGANIZATIONS

Advocates for Youth
1025 Vermont Ave., NW, #200
Washington, DC 20005
(202) 347-5700
www.advocatesforyouth.org
www.youthresource.com

BiNet USA
4201 Wilson Blvd, No. 110-311
Arlington, VA 22203
(202) 986-7186
www.binetusa.org

Bisexual Resource Center
PO Box 1026
Boston, MA 02117-1026
(617) 424-9595
www.biresource.org

Gay Asian Pacific Support Network
PO Box 461104
Los Angeles, Ca 90046
(213) 368-6488
www.gapsn.org

Gay and Lesbian Medical Association
459 Fulton St., #107
San Francisco, Ca 94102
(415) s255-4547
www.glma.org

Gender Education and Advocacy
PO Box 65
Kensington, MD 20895
(301) 949-3822
www.gender.org

GenderPAC
1638 R. St., NW, #100
Washington, DC 20009-6446
(202) 462-6610
www.gpac.org

GLAAD
(Gay and Lesbian Alliance Against Defamation)
1825 Connecticut Avenue NW, 5th Floor
Washington, DC 20009
(202) 986-1360
(202) 667-0902 fax
(800) GAY-MEDIA
www.glaad.org

GLSEN
(Gay, Lesbian, and Straight Education Network)
121 West 27th Street, Suite 804
New York, NY 10001
(212) 727-0135
(212) 727-0254
www.glsen.org

HRC
(Human Rights Campaign)
919 18th Street NW
Washington, DC 20006
(202) 628-4160
(202) 347-5323
www.hrc.org

International Foundation for Gender Education
PO Box 540229
Waltham, MA 02454-0229
(781) 899-2212
www.ifge.org

Lesbian and Gay Immigration Rights Task Force
230 Park Ave. #904
New York, NY 10169
(212) 818-9639
www.lgirtf.org

The LGBT Community Center National History Archive
208 West 13th Street
New York, NY 10011
(212) 620-7310
www.gaycenter.org/archives

Mautner Project for Lesbians With Cancer
1707 L. St., NW #500
Washington, DC 20036
(202) 332-5536
www.mautnerproject.org

National Association of Lesbian, Gay, Bisexual & Transgender Community Centers
208 W. 13th St.
New York, NY 10011
(212) 620-7310
www.gaycenter.org/natctr

National Association of People With AIDS
1413 K St, NW 7th Floor
Washington, DC 20005
(202) 898-0414
www.napwa.org

National Black Lesbian and Gay Leadership Forum
1714 Franklin St, #100-140
Oakland, CA 94612
(510) 302-0930

National Center for Lesbian Rights
870 Market St, #570
San Francisco, CA 94102
(415) 392-9257
www.nclrights.org

National Gay and Lesbian Task Force
1700 Kalorama Rd. NW
Washington, DC 20009-2624
(202) 332-6483
www.ngltf.org

National Latina/o Lesbian, Gay, Bisexual & Transgender Organization (LLEGO)
1420 K St., NW #200
Washington, DC 20006
(202) 408-5380
www.llego.org

National Minority AIDS Council
1931 13th St., NW
Washington, DC 20009
(202) 483-6622
www.nmac.org

National Youth Advocacy Coalition
1638 R. St., NW, #300
Washington, DC 20009
(202) 319-7596
www.nyacyouth.org

ONE Institute & Archives
909 West Adams Boulevard
Los Angeles, CA 90007
(213) 741-0094
www.oneinstitute.org

Parents, Families, and Friends of Lesbians and Gays
1101 14th Street NW, Suite 1030
Washington, DC 20005
(202) 638-4200
(202) 638-0243 fax
www.pflag.org

Project Angel Food
7574 Sunset Boulevard
Los Angeles, CA 9004
(323) 845-1800
www.angelfood.org

Servicemembers Legal Defense Network
PO Box 65301
Washington, DC 20035-5301
(202) 328-3244
www.sldn.org

Sexuality Information and Education Council of the United States
130 W. 42nd St, #350
New York, NY 10036-7802
(212) 819-9770
www.siecus.org

Queer Youth TV
10573 West Pico Boulevard, #606
Los Angeles, CA 90064
www.queeryouthTV.org
E-mail: bret@queeryouthTV.org

HATE CRIMES PREVENTION

The National Center for Hate Crime Prevention Education Development Center, Inc.
55 Chapel Street
Newton, MA 02158-1060
(617) 969-7100
(617) 244-3436 fax
(800) 225-4276
www.edc.org/HHD/hatecrime

National Youth Violence Prevention Resource Center
(866) 723-3968
301-562-1001 fax
(800) 243-7012
301-562-1001 fax

Simon Wiesenthal Center
1399 South Roxbury Drive
Los Angeles, California 90035
www.wiesenthal.org

Southern Poverty Law Center
400 Washington Avenue
Montgomery, AL 36104
www.splcenter.org

HIV/AIDS INFORMATION

The HIV/AIDS Treatment Information Service (ATIS)
Central resource for federally approved treatment guidelines for HIV and AIDS.
(800) 448-0440
www.hivatis.org

The NAMES Project AIDS Memorial
Quilt Website
www.aidsquilt.org

TB/HIV Research Laboratory
Dedicated to research into prevention and treatment of TB and HIV.
www.brown.edu/Research

The Safer Sex Page
www.safersex.org

The Center for Disease Control
www.cdc.gov

The Joint United Nations Programme on AIDS (UNAIDS)
Advocate for global action on HIV/AIDS.
www.unaids.org

The Queer Resources Director of AIDS/HIV Information
www.qrd.org

Rural Prevention Center
Joint project of Indiana University and Purdue University for the study and promotion of HIV/STD prevention.
www.indiana.edu/~aids

The Biology of AIDS: Compiled Resources
AIDS research directory
www.affirmation.org

CAPS
The Center for AIDS Prevention Studies at the University of California, San Francisco
www.caps.ucsf.edu

RELIGIOUS ORGANIZATIONS

Affirmation (Mormon)
PO Box 46022
Los Angeles, Ca 90046-0022
(323) 255-7251
www.affirmation.org

Affirmation (United Methodist)
PO Box 1021
Evanston, IL 60204
(847) 733-9590
www.umairm.org

Al-Fatiha Foundation (Muslim)
405 Park Ave., #1500
New York, NY 10022
(212) 752-4242
www.al-fatiha.net

Association of Welcoming and Affirming Baptists
PO Box 2596
Attleboro Falls, MA 02763-0894
(508) 226-1945
www.wabaptists.org

Brethren/Mennonite Council For Lesbian and Gay Concerns
PO Box 6300
Minneapolis, MN 55406
(612) 722-6906
www.webcom.com/bmc/welcom.html

Dignity/USA (Catholic)
1500 Massachusetts Ave., NW #11
Washington, DC 20005-1894
(800) 877-8797
www.dignityusa.org

Emergence International (Christian Scientist)
PO Box 2627
Phoenix, AZ 85068
(800) 280-6653
www.cslesbigay.org/emergence

Evangelicals Concerned with Reconciliation
PO Box 19734
Seattle, WA 98109-6734
www.ecwr.org

Gay Buddhist Fellowship
2215-R Market St., #162
San Francisco, Ca 94114
(415) 207-8113
www.gaybuddhist.org

Integrity (Episcopalian)
1718 M St., NW
PO Box 148
Washington, DC 20036
(202) 462-9193
www.inegrityusa.org

Lutherans Concerned
PO Box 1022
Indianapolis, IN 46206-1922
www.lcna.org

More Light Presbyterians
369 Montezuma Ave., #447
Santa Fe, NM 87501-2626
(505) 820-7082
www.mlp.org

National Gay Pentecostal Alliance
PO Box 20428
Ferndale, MI 48220
www.ameritech.net/users
lighthse84/ngpa.html

Office of GLBT Concerns for Unitarian Universalists Association
25 Beacon St.
Boston, MA 02108
(617) 948-6475
www.uua.org/obgltc

SDA Kinship International
(Seventh Day Adventist)
PO Box 7320
Laguna Niguel, CA 92607
(949) 248-1299
www.sdakinship.org

United Fellowship of Metropolitan Community Churches
8704 Santa Monica Blvd, 2nd Floor
West Hollywood, CA 90069
(310) 360-8640
www.ufmcc.com

World Congress of Gay and Lesbian Jewish Organizations
PO Box 23379
Washington, DC 20026-3379
(202) 452-7424
www.wcgljo.org

Unity Fellowship Church Movement
(African American)
5148 West Jefferson Blvd.
Los Angeles, CA 90016
(323) 938-8322
www.nmha.org

SUICIDE PREVENTION

American Foundation for Suicide Prevention
www.AFSP.org
Hotline service of the national Hopeline Network.
Links callers to local crisis centers.
(800) SUICIDE

Trevor Helpline (for GLBT youth)
(800) 850-8078

National Mental Health Association
1021 Prince Street
Alexandria, VA 22314-2971
(703) 684-7722
(703) 684-5968 fax
www.nmha.org

Mental Health Information Center
(800) 969-NMHA
TTY Line 800-433-5959

Youth Violence and Suicide Prevention Team—National Center for Injury Prevention and Control
4770 Buford Highway, MS K-60
Atlanta, GA 30341
(770) 488-4646
www.cdc.gov/ncipc

The Jason Foundation, Inc.— suicide awareness and prevention
www.jasonfoundation.com
(888) 881-2323

The National Suicide Helpline
(800) SUICIDE

The National "YOUTH" Crisis Helpline
(800) 999-9999

NDMDA—National Depressive/Manic Depressive Association
(800) 826-3632

National Resource Center for Suicide Prevention and Aftercare
(404) 256-9797

American Foundation for Suicide Prevention
(888) 333-2377

Suicide Prevention Advocacy Network
www.spanusa.org

National Depression Screening Project
To locate a free, confidential
screening site near you call
(800) 573-4433

National Mental Health Association—
treatment referrals and services
(800) 969-NMHA(6642)

Suicide Information & Education Center
(403) 245-3900

Norman Institute—gender orientation
(816) 960-7200

Friends for Survival—survivor line
(916) 392-0664

Compassionate Friends—parent grief
(630) 990-0010

PeopleColorAgainstSuicide
(512) 245-2113

Prospect Publishing
www.prospectpublishing.com

Public Interest Productions
www.publicinterestprods.org

Randi Driscoll
www.randidriscoll.com

University of Wyoming
www.uwyo.edu

United Against Hate
www.unitedagainsthate.com

ADDITIONAL WEB SITES

Cire Foundation
www.cirefoundation.org

Gay.com
www.gay.com

Matthew Shepard Foundation
www.matthewshepard.org

PlanetOut.Com
www.planetout.com

CONTRIBUTORS

Photographers

Alex Gibson fell in love with photography when she realized that she could record a moment of reality on film. In 1996 Gibson began photographing the lives of the homeless in Mexico and America. Since 1999 she has been capturing gay life for many publications, especially Southern California's *Frontiers* Newsmagazine. She was able to combine both fields of work in 2001 when she collaborated with the Matthew Shepard Foundation and CIRE to photograph *Out In The Cold*, a documentary on homeless queer youth. This photo exhibit now travels worldwide as a forum for truth and education. It is her hope that through her work the often nameless and faceless people in this world may find a voice.

Nanette Martin is a professional, editorial photographer based in Denver, Colorado. She currently contracts with *People* magazine and is involved in several ongoing documentary projects that address cultural, societal, and environmental issues. Her image of a protestor at Matthew Shepard's funeral in Laramie, Wyoming was featured in *Life* magazine.

Jay Wheeler is a Los Angeles based photographer specializing in sports, fashion and action photography. His passion for social change compelled him to contribute to *A Face in the Crowd* and he has volunteered his services for numerous non-profit human rights organizations.

Kelly Wine is a native Southern Californian. He has been taking photographs since the 1970's as a natural extension of his creating art. Kelly has worked as an artist since 1986, doing fine art, freelance illustration, and 2-D/3-D computer game artwork. Kelly has enjoyed photographically documenting gay rights protests that have taken place around Los Angeles, San Francisco, Orange County, and San Diego. He lives in Santa Monica with his partner Joe of four years.

Albert J. Winn is a photographer whose work has been shown internationally and is included in the permanent collection of. among others, the Library of Congress (Washington, D.C.), the Jewish Museum (New York), and Light Work (Syracuse, NY). He was awarded a fellowship from the National Endowment for the Arts / Western States Arts Federation, for *My Life Until Now,* photographs and stories, and a fellowship from the Memorial Foundation for Jewish Culture. He was included in *Made in California: 1900-2000* (LACMA) and received his MFA from the California Institute of the Arts.

Additional photographs provided courtesy from the following:

Ismail Elshareef	Judy Lawne	Alan Skinner
Cheryl Haines	Rob Lebow	Eric Stephen Jacobs
Alexandra Hedison	Martha Murphy	Claudia Wong
David La Chapelle	Rhea Murray	

Additional content provided by the following organizations and individuals:

Eric Criswell, founder of the CIRE Foundation, in association with Judy Shepard and the Matthew Shepard Foundation, produced the documentary film, *Out in the Cold*. Many of the photographs of homeless youth that were collected for this documentary, along with other personal stories, are featured in *A Face in the Crowd*. Photographs were taken by Alex Gibson. To learn more about the CIRE Foundation, please visit their website www.cirefoundation.org.

Randi Driscoll went to her piano to find solace in my music after learning of the murder of Matthew Shepard. What transpired was "What Matters," a song about his life, his family and the unconditional love they represent. Proceeds from the sale of this single are donated to the Matthew Shepard Foundation. Limited copies of *A Face in the Crowd* can be purchased with this beautiful song written and performed by Randi Driscoll. For more information, please visit her website at www.randidriscoll.com.

The Gay Lesbian and Straight Education Network (GLSEN) envisions a future in which every child learns to respect and accept all people, regardless of sexual orientation or gender identity. GLSEN works in collaboration with Judy Shepard and the Matthew Shepard Foundation, in addition to being a valuable resource for statistical information and provided content on the Day of Silence Project found in *A Face in the Crowd*.

The Lesbian, Gay, Bisexual and Transgender Community Center, National History Archive works to preserve our communities' heritage, making it accessible through regular exhibits, publications and scholarly research activities. Founded and coordinated by volunteer archivist Rich Wandel, the collection includes thousands of papers, periodicals, correspondence, and photographs donated by lesbian, gay, bisexual and transgender individuals and organizations. Historical images can be found in the pages of *A Face in the Crowd*.

Project Angel Food is a daily meal delivery program for men, women, and children who are disabled by HIV/AIDS. Meals, prepared by professional chefs and volunteer assistants, are attractive, nutritious and always made with the freshest ingredients. Registered dietitians provide clients with individual, nutritional counseling. There is no charge to clients for these services and since its inception in 1989, Project Angel Food has prepared and delivered more than 2.5 million meals. Volunteers from this nonprofit organization are featured in *A Face in the Crowd*.

Queer Youth TV is a non-profit organization with the mission to provide information for lesbian, gay, bisexual and transgender (LGBT) youth and the general public through original Internet video content that promotes a critical understanding of LGBT culture, institutions, topics and issues. Queer Youth TV was conceived as an Internet "safe zone" by Bret Berg in December 2000 in response to the lack of substantial non-commercial web resources for LGBT youth. Excerpts from Queer Youth TV's "Coming-Out Project" are featured in *A Face in the Crowd*.

PHOTOGRAPHY CREDITS

Coming-out stories & photos
Courtesy of Bret Berg, Queer Youth TV
19, 26, 33, 42, 51, 60, 67, 72, 81, 84, 91, 96, 108, 113, 116

Ismail Elshareef
88

Alex Gibson
50, 112, 115

Homeless youth editorial & photos by Alex Gibson
Courtesy of Eric Criswell of the CIRE Foundation
16, 17, 20, 23, 28, 31, 34, 37, 38, 41, 48, 53, 54, 57, 58, 61, 64, 66, 68, 78, 83, 86, 89, 90, 93, 94, 97, 102, 105, 106, 111, 114, 117, 122

Photos provided courtesy of GLSEN
101, 106, 107, 109, 110, 122

Donated by Barbara Warren & Stephanie Grant
Courtesy of the LGBT Community Center National History Archive
46

Cheryl Haines
54, 55

Alexandra Hedison
IX

Eric Stephen Jacobs
Courtesy of the LGBT Community Center National History Archive
47

David LaChapelle
125

Judy Lawne
38

Rob Lebow of The Cimarron Group
Courtesy of Project Angel Food
52, 53

Nanette Martin
21, 22, 23, 27, 28, 31, 34, 36, 56, 57. 70, 71, 79, 82, 85, 86, 87, 90, 94, 97

Martha Murphy
39

Courtesy of Rhea Murray
15, 93

Alan Skinner
Courtesy of Queer Youth TV
121

Photo from the Frank Thompson collection
Courtesy of the LGBT Community Center National History Archive
73

Jay Wheeler
17, 18, 24, 25, 29, 32, 35, 40, 41, 48, 49, 59, 61, 66, 68, 80

Kelly Wine
77, 102, 103, 104, 105

Albert J. Winn
43, 62, 63, 64, 65

Claudia Wong
Courtesy of Crossroads School
117, 118, 119